John Hegley currently resides close to his North London birthplace. Educated in Luton, Bristol and Bradford University. Joined Interaction community arts collective in 1978, and has subsequently continued their interactive ethos. Early '80s John Peel Sessions with the Popticians began a series of broadcasts across the radio network which suggests a varied palette and appeal. Has produced twelve books, two albums and one mug. Once performed at a Colombian women's prison. Has not been asked back.

PEACE, LOVE & POTATOES

John Hegley

with drawings largely by the author

This paperback edition published in 2017
First published in 2012 by Serpent's Tail,
an imprint of Profile Books Ltd
3 Holford Yard
Bevin Way
London WC1X 9HD
www.serpentstail.com

ISBN 978 1 78125 838 5
eISBN 978 1 84765 873 9

Designed and typeset by sue@lambledesign.demon.co.uk
Printed by CPI Group (UK) Ltd, Croydon CRO 4YY

10 9 8 7 6 5 4 3 2 1

Contents

Acknowledgements

'An Alien Address' was originally written as an exposition to aliens about human modes of transport for Mel Brimfield's show at Collective gallery in Edinburgh. 'An Anatomy of Injury' was for a collection of performances with anatomical connections, curated by Clod Ensemble. 'Morris' and 'Mike's Muse' were originally published on *Guardian* Online. 'An ending of the reoffending', 'The Last Skimpot Flyer', and 'Art in Melbourne' appeared in *The Iron Book of New Humorous Verse*, and an earlier version of 'Another Poem for Eve to Mark Out of Ten' appeared in *The Ropes*.

'Blood Donor' was composed in the nineties for a campaign encouraging the giving of blood. 'Alternatives to losing your temper' was written and performed at a forum on domestic violence at the Quad in Derby. 'Let Us Play' was a Valentine's card commission for the Brunel Engine House Museum in Rotherhithe.

The Dickens poem was a response to a call for writings about the great author for the collection *A Mutual Friend*. Jake Arnott, it was, who told me of audiences asking Mr Dickens not to tell his tale of Nancy. 'Keeping Mummy' first appeared in the magazine *Magma*, the poetry hotbed. The John Keats pieces came out of a residency at Keats House in Hampstead.

My gratitude to editors Lisa Owens and Ruthie Petrie, to Sam Humphreys who originally commissioned the volume, and to Robert Kirby, my literary agent, who found the book this home at Serpent's Tail.

The volume's title acknowledges the fine, sane song by Nick Lowe, '(What's so funny about) peace, love and understanding?'. And thank you to Andy Ching, Vicky Hueber, Pat Pickles, Anne Edyvean, Eleanor Moreton and Pam Brabants on the Kiwi side. And I'll think of more... Keith Moore, for one.

An alien address

Do you have bendy buses
or are you jet-propelled?
Do you have those dangly ball things on tube trains,
to be held onto when it's crowded,
I don't know what they're called?
How much is there in your world, that you haven't got
    a name for?
Is it the stars you aim for?
Do you ever get appalled,
when your brand new central heating has been
    shoddily installed
by a bunch of cowboys?
Are you green, are you translucent,
do you have any pets?
Do you have mental illness
or menthol cigarettes?
Do you ever feel you don't fit in with all the rest?
Do you feel like an outsider,
like a money spider in a nest
of penniless termites?
Do you ever say 'To be honest'?
Do you ever say 'For my sins'?

Or are truthfulness and repentance where another
        world begins?
Do your bins get emptied on a Tuesday?
Do you have three-legged races
you can compete in on your own?
Do you have stripy deck chairs that get wind blown
when they're vacant?
Is there anybody out there?
Have you got ears for this?
Have you got liver tablets,
or the equivalent of Bristol?
Do you wear a pair of glasses, for maybe you
        have eyes?
Do you start off as a baby and then increase in size,
but lose your sense of wonderment in the process?
Do you ever get on a crowded train
and have to put your luggage in the vestibule
and do you ever sit in the seat nearest the door
so you can keep an eye on it
and then more people get on
and you have to stand up and say
'Excuse me, but could you move out of the way, please,
I cannot see my luggage'?

Defoe and de friendly Finnish

My dad read me *Robinson Crusoe*.
The book cost a couple of bob,
and Bob was the name of my father,
in the home and the clerical job.
Crusoe – adventure's main crony,
the impression that alien made
making the most of the island
in his customised stockade.
Those nights of that bedroom retelling
Robinson Crusoe, the bold
with me and my dad, glad to know him
enthralled as we hauled up our gold
from the chest that my father would open:
the book he would look at and hold.

The Moomins, I share with my daughter.
We've room for their busy and joke.
They live in a world that is distant,
even the grumpier 'Groke'
has its endearing features.
The creatures are all co-existent.
They get on with separate lives.
And even when there is a conflict,

3

the pen of the author contrives
a reasonable resolution,
at least in the stories we've read:
a peaceable stand-off of some sort, a remembering that
    the world is never short of incredible.

If the Moomins met Robinson Crusoe,
perhaps they could help him to see
that not every threat to your world picture
is an enemy.

Bob a job

My dad he was *Bob* in the office, René is the way he
    began,
but René didn't stay, he got hidden away and England
    knew a different man.

There's bits of ourselves
that get put onto shelves.
There's shadows that we don't ever show.
Bob, he was so undercover he didn't even let himself
    know.

His mum being a dancer with the Folies Bergère
it was something he didn't disclose,
the only thing we had that was French in our pad,
    apart from our dad,
was the windows.

My daddy had a secret identity in the manner of a
    Superhero.

Bob in the office and *Bob* in the tie.
It just made it easier for him getting by.

Bob said goodbye to the onions and brie,
the tongue of his mother, it wasn't to be.
He was fluent, but truant, eventually,
but I remember way back when he sang 'Frère Jacques'
     to me.

My dad he was *Bob* in the office
but, earlier on in his life,
René is the name that he dug into the bench
in Paris, with his penknife.
And not Bob.

Many happy returns

On fifty years of Luton Central Library

Friday afternoon.
School holiday in the summer.
In town.
Mum in the shops,
my sister Angela and I
under the shelf-life spell of the spines.

Each of us, hunting down our permitted quartet of
    titles.
Angie-Boo is a Doctor Doolittle fan
and we both want Billy Bunter.
Alongside the vitals, we'll take a punt on an unknown
to bolster our under-arm holdings.
I strike gold, as I add to my hoard
Marianne Dreams and Ian Serrailier's *Silver Sword*.

As we delve shelve-wise
we'll chance upon each other in an aisle
and then resume our searching.
in amongst the upright-tightly-lined-along-and-
    clearly-indexed
perching.

And with our gathered-up pilings
we get sat at a Readers' table
and in amongst the low-slung voices,
we dive into our choices
until Mum bag-ladies in from the outside world,
smiling
and taking
us home

from home.

At a reading in Rotheram library

To the Wednesday night Rotherham Library audience,
I am describing myself back at ten years old.
I tell them how we climbed over an old garden wall
and went scrumping apples.
Then I ask
'Do you say "scrumping" up here,
or do you have a different word for it?'
A woman at the back answers,
'Aye, we do have another word for it:
Theft.'

An ending of the re-offending

For the prisoner paying the price
just a punishment may not suffice.
The best use of time
may be learning to rhyme,
making sure that it isn't too nice
a process of course.
You don't want people thinking a life of crime
leads to loads of free poetry workshops.

Dear Earwig,

I haven't seen you for over a year, now. Maybe two.
I wonder what's the longest time I've gone without
seeing you? Where have you been, Earwig? Sometimes
seen around a plughole, but rarely round a lughole.
I hope you've not gone all extinct like some birds have
– your flame extinguished, your name no more than
a name with nothing to call it to. Earwig, you may be
small, but the world wouldn't be as big without you.

I remember seeing you scarpering along for the first
time. I was with my dad. Maybe I was four. You seemed
funny and a bit scary, but because dad was there, I
wasn't too frightened. He seemed glad to see you –
maybe because you are a bit funny. Maybe because
he was glad to tell me a new word, a new insect, a
bit more about our world. I always smile when I see
you, now – unless I'm depressed. There will always be
something of my dad in you, but with more legs.

Love,
John

11

Art appreciation

I walked round the Liverpool Tate.
There were rocks there of withering weight.
They meant little to me
but then, I couldn't see
them with the same intimate understanding of
whoever got landed with the job of lugging them
in there.

In Aberdeen Museum and Art Gallery, I came upon
an exhibit which angered me. 'A sleeping bag!' I
exclaimed, inward indignant. 'So they just lie out a
sleeping bag on the floor and that's a "Work" of Art,
is it?' And then I look at the label. *Gavin Turk. Sleeping
Bag: Bronze.*

Pablo and Georges squaring up

Pablo and Georges, a while before the radio;
regularly in and out
of each other's studio.
Each is an artist.
Each is a Cubist.
Pablo's a Spaniard, Georges a man of France.
With brushes for their batons
they both conduct a square dance.
The world it gets squared up to,
the fragmentation it gets done
and with the world safely in pieces,
the two men dine as one
like Gilbert and George:
Pablo and Georges.

The manner of their meeting,
circa 1904:
Georges saw some of Pablo's stuff
and wanted to see more.
And maybe he went 'Phwoar!'
The two had stuff in common
like the future, he felt sure
and going round to Pablo's,

through the door he put a message.
The text it was predictive
and very, very short:
'To our undiscovered memories'
or something of the sort.
It's early morning in Paris
and the shutters fold away.
For Pablo and Georges
it's another gorgeous Cubist day,
going for broke with the ochre and the grey.
I see the duo sitting in their lairs.
Sitting on their art-directors' chairs.
Trying to take each other unawares.
Paying all their homages to the squares.
Pablo will become fablo,
how his future's set to flare.
But will he ever be any happier
than he was back there,
When it was Pablo and Georges?
Georges and Pablo.
All square.

Paris 1904

Grandad's song requesting Grandma's hand (and feet) in marriage

To the tune of the Can Can, perhaps

I have come over to France from England where we
    like to dance
the Morris dance, a different dance, from dances I have
    seen you doing.
Seeing you doing your dance,
how it improves my existence.
Just to have a single glance, I'd gladly spend the
    summer queuing.
You can move me from stagnation, any time of any
    day.
You improve me, when my smile
is miles and miles and miles and miles and miles and
    miles away.
You can make me feel I'm zoomy
when I'm catacomby,
you can make my trials seem like they're a trifle.
When it seems the world would stifle,
you can make me Eiffel

I am very happy to report.
You can make me want to leave the country of my
    upbringing
to start anew in somewhere where I hardly know the
    lingo,
although, luckily my mother was a Frenchwoman
so she has taught me some of it
but you can teach me all of it,
all the words and how they fit,
the whole of it,
you can familiarise me with every little bit of it.
You can make it all seem thrilling,
you are the full shilling, you're fulfilling my existence
    thank you kindly.
You can make me feel I'm conger, when I feel no longer
than a maggot that is very short.
You can put flavour in my flan.
Can, can put body in my bran.
Can we be one woman and man?
Please do say 'Oui'
so that we can
begin to plan
what we can do
me and un canny you.

Let us play

Let's dig tunnels.
Let's build bridges.
Let's get close
like clouds of midges.
What was under
Mr Brunel's hat?
His love-letters
And his sand*widges*.
Let us cross that big divide.
Let us go and coincide.
And with the space between deducted,
Let us mind what's been constructed.

You provide the motion and I'll start the debate.
You provide the provender and I'll supply the napkin
    and the plate.
Let's combine this life of mine with your own slender
    fate.
Let me elaborate.
Let's be thick as thieves can be.
Let's thicken up the ice and then entice the world to
    skate.
You be narrow, I'll be straight.

You be weight and I'll be volume.
Let's make a pair of zeros
make a bigger figure eight.
Let's collaborate.

Their expectations of Christmas were rather different
(M. Brimfield)

I have at home my father's invitation to meet the founder of the Scouting movement, Lord Baden-Powell, in Paris, 1920. Printed on card, smaller than a postcard, larger than a calling card, with the invitees named in what I assume to be fountain pen ink: 'Hegley and friends'. He was fifteen at the time, and he was in the English Scout troop in Paris. His father was English and a certain Englishness was seen as his son's rightful inheritance.

I have wondered whether my father got to make the engagement, and if so, with whom. There is a photograph from the period, with him wearing his uniform and holding his wooden Scout staff. Did that staff accompany him? Does it still exist? Did he think of it as a friend?

PARIS 1922: PREPARING FOR THE FIRST NIGHT OF THE BOY SCOUT PANTO

Scenes between my father (René Robert) and his mother (Maman)

René Robert Maman!

Maman In English, Robert. You KNOW your father wants English spoken in the home.

René R Sorry, Mother. I'm just over-excited about tonight's performance. I cannot find my garters.

Maman That sounds like something I might have said when I was with the Folies Bergère... 'Where are my garters Kiki'... 'I don't know, Koko.'

René R Who are Kiki and Koko, Mother?

Maman They are the beautiful dancing girls who were once your godmother Mireille and I. Our stage names. Our wage names... Look! You are WEARING your garters, Robert.

René R That's because I'm so excited, I don't know what's going on.

Maman Well, let me tell you what is going on... and our lovely audience, also. I am French. It is Paris. We are a little after Christmas. I am married to Henri Robert, an Englishman with French blood, but an Englishman. He lives in France and it is agreed that our child will be a child of both cultures and tongues. Hence our boy is a member of the English Scout troop, speaks English in the home and *Français, à l'ecôle*. If you'll excuse my French.

René R Of course, Mum. Right, I'll just put on my woggle and then I am ready.

Maman I don't know the French for woggle? And if I did I wouldn't use it in the house. Are there really to be 40 thieves in the production, Robert?

René R Yes, Mother, some of the Scouts from the American troop are taking part in the production.

Maman And YOU were single-handedly responsible for the scene-painting.

René R Do you think Monsieur Braque will appear tonight? Do you think he will appreciate my handiwork? He only likes the queer stuff.

Maman In fairness, Georges only likes the GOOD stuff and if your stuff is good, he will say so.

René R Our Scoutmaster says my street looks real.

Drawing of Dad scene-painting by R. M. Hegley, with onlooker (after Matisse) by J. R. Hegley

Maman   I think Georges might say we can leave the real for reality.

René R   Mother, may we take the tram to the performance?

Maman   But it is only three stops?

René R   I love the tram, Mother.
I love the people lulled into half slumber by the rocking.
I love the rattle on the way of gleaming iron.
I love the ticketing designed so clear and simple.
I love the worn-ness of the pouch of the conductor.

I love the pattern which is woven in the
     seating.
I love the cigarette smoke battling with the
     perfume.
I love to stare out at the street names of our
     quarter
I love...

Maman ALRIGHT, Robert! We will take the tram.

POST PANTO PERFORMANCE AT THE
REFRESHMENT TABLE

Probably spoken in English

Maman I have spoken with Georges.

René R   ... and what did he think, Mother? He has seen our performance, what are his thoughts?

Maman   He thinks that the refreshment table offers a poor choice of sandwiches.

René R   But did he mention the scene painting?

Maman   He says that the street looks so real he could walk up it.

René R   But I didn't think Monsieur Braque liked paintings that make things look real.

Maman   He did not say that he liked it, Robert.

Being is believing

I believe in you.
I believe in you
being close to me.
I believe in you being close to me
intimately.
I believe in you being close to me
intimately, regularly.
I believe in you being close to me
intimately, regularly,
just not today.
I believe in you being close to me
intimately, regularly
just not today
because sometimes
I need to be with myself alone
all the better to be with you
more intimately.

Steam shipped

My grandma and my grandfather they parted.
The wherefores and the whys, I do not know,
but Grandma took the boat
out to the transatlantic world
and she didn't have to row, luckily.

The steamship pushes out of the French harbour,
the year is circa 1923.
My grandma, dad and auntie
have said *au revoir* to France
and they advance towards their chances in the land of
 the Cherokee.
The steamship's going steaming to another world,
looking back you learn the lack of home.
The steamship's going steaming to a transatlantic
 world,
a boat
that wrote
a farewell note
on several thousand miles
of swelling foam.

From Paris to New York.
From the boulevard to the sidewalk.
Where the game is pool,
where you don't fool around with boules.

The steamship pushes into New York harbour.
The skyscrapers, a blur in the morning haze,
My grandma, dad and auntie,
a little spree of three French *émigrés*,
seeking out the new speakeasy days.
My granny's going to dance on American stages.
She's going to get paid in American wages.
She's going to spend her bucks in the land of the
      candy store,
where the word is 'Shucks!'
Where you don't say *'Zut alors!'*
Anymore.

Rothko

In the Rothko room,
the Rothko room,
I sense I'm sat in a catacomb.
In the Rothko room,
the Rothko room,
a sense of something you might exhume.
In the Rothko room,
the Rothko room,
the floating blues and purples loom.
In the Rothko room
the Rothko room,
you get a sense of suspending doom.
In the Rothko room
the Rothko room,
they're side by slide
like a bride and gloom.

But, then there's the yellow ones.

1930 ON THE TRAM, NEW YORK

(nearly all in English)

Robert   Well, one thing that hasn't changed in the
seven years since we left France, Mom, is the
pleasure I take from the tram journey.

Mother   Don't call me MOM!... America has certainly
enriched us, Robert, but,
I miss my mother tongue
I miss my mother country
I miss my mother
and I miss my *citron pressé*.

Robert   It's the straw which broke the camel's back.

Mother   That's it... that's it, Robert!
C'est la goutte d'eau qui fait déborder la vase.
I have had enough!

Robert   Mother, your eye has sprung a leak. Please
take my handkerchief and dab it.

Mother   This country has given us a good living, but I
am ready to give it up. It is time to go home.

Robert   And I will return with you. What will become
of me, I wonder?

Mother   I will tell you what will become of you, Robert.
You will live in Nice, because your gran has

moved there and she is old and she needs us. And you will find a great peace, and you will paint your native country with a passion and aplomb. And you will be happy in the country of your birth and you will tread its earth and streets so gratefully, but after eight years of such happiness, you will head for the shores and the trams of England. And please attempt to write to your mother.

Seaside fun, 1931

Spring and spray on the English coast,
the sun says I'll be here all day
it's not an idle boast.
And two little girls who live in the town
are heading for the beach now each has got her toast
    and cocoa down.
One's my mum and one's her sister.
Ivy and Gladys, off they scram.
Ivy and Gladys, 'Don't slam the door!'
Ivy and Gladys heading for
the side of the sea which they adore,
in Ramsgate.

What'll become of Gladys and Mum?
Mummy, she will have the three
with a pint-size piece of the *Fleur de Lys*.
And Gladys, she will skate on ice
and live in four nice wooden walls
beside the world's most famous Falls
but that's all far from this silent Charleston age
when hats were in
and twelve and threepence halfpenny
was a decent working wage.

Ivy and Gladys in the sand.
Ivy and Gladys by the bandstand.
Ivy and Gladys in the garden of England.

Open-topping on the trams
Ivy and Gladys close as clams, in Ramsgate.

My Riviera father
my Kentish coastal mum,
they have the sea in common
and each other yet to come.

Glad all over

Down to work

Dad returned to France from America around 1930.
We still have some of his land and seascapes, paintings
from the time: they are conventional, accomplished
and cheery works. He had the idea to create some of
them with papier-mâché foliage in the foreground. He
told me this was his own invention, by which he meant
he had invented foreground papier-mâché foliage. I
was later to tell my teacher, Sister Mary Lucia, that
my dad had invented papier-mâché and Sister said to
me, 'I don't think your father *did* invent papier-mâché,
John.' It was not said unkindly, but it was a wounding,
a doubt's shadow cast upon the infallible.

Sister

Back in the days of black and white TV
Sister Mary Lucia wore black and white
as sported by The Hatters, that is Luton Town, the
    football club,
unless you're a supporter of the other team called
    Hatters
from much further north in England:
Stockport County.

Sister Mary Lucia got us to pray, when our school day
was almost over, so that we could thank the ones
who looked over our shoulders, the upholders of the
    truth and trusting,
who helped us get our bearings
in a world
of hats, ball-bearings, aeroplanes
and many Vauxhall Motors.
Our angels.

Sister Mary Lucia taught us the song that we would sing
to give us a belonging sense,
to make us feel more strong than tense,
reminding us from whence we came,

reminding us that when we came into this world,
we were hurled here with our angels.

She wore a dove of silver,
and gave us pieces of her mind.
And she told us of the love of those
who stood there in the wings, behind us.
Our Angels.

Sister Mary Lucia made calendars from cardboard, for
  selling at the Christmas school bazaar.
My Dad gave me the cardboard, which he got from
  work, to give her.
Sister Mary Lucia, I told her that I loved her
even though she sent me down to join the Baby's Class
for acting like a baby, maybe that would make me
  think again,
a little bit of pain and doing my addition with a baby's
  pencil for a while
the smile wiped off my fallen features
but not wiped from the features of my angels.

All the time spent at Saint Josephs, I could really sense
  the sacred,
seven largely happy years, with heaven just a short
  distance away
but at eleven, I had seen the last of Sister Mary Lucia
and it seemed that the angelic had gone on holiday.
  And I missed her.

The sacred and myself would see a lot of separation,
although, sometimes on a railway station
I would sense some peace
and on my travels on occasion, the unravelling
        persuasion
and the passion of a people
saw my ration of the sacredness increase:
in New Zealand and in Greece and also, just outside of
        Grimsby. (At Healing Academy, funnily enough.)
And on the terraces at football.
Unification and release.

Sister said we all had angels.
Our baby sisters, guardians and grans.
Even the Watford fans.

She had a dove made out of silver,
as did all the other Sisters in their veils.
And, I told her that I loved her,
Sister Mary Lucia, from Wales.

She took the cardboard given by my father,
my father, who was native of Paree.
And she acquainted us with the saints and with
        our angels
Sister Mary Lucia,
Merci.

VIEUX NICE

38

Verse inspired by Dad's painting of La Rue de la Providence

With thanks to Henry Longfellow

Here he is, his job is cobbler,
dealing with the soles of people.
Healing soles his occupation.
People hear through words of mouthing,
he is first in terms of lasting.
They are sure he knows his business.
There's no need for advertising.
There's no board above his practice.
People know of his perfection,
like the stooping woman climbing
slowly up uneven stepping.
She may need to hold the railing
but, she also keeps on gripping
life and all its many pathways.
We can hear her inner-speaking,
'These are steps we climbed as children
stepping long and so light-footed
now I take my time to do it
like I've so much time remaining.'

Then, around the Old Town corner,
not so distant from this dreamer
there's another woman walking.
She's a visitor from Lima.
Has she got an armadillo?
She is carrying a parcel.
What is held within, I wonder?
Maybe footwear, nicely mended.
Maybe there's an armadillo.
Maybe you have got an answer?
She goes down the ancient alley,
down towards the sitting youngster,
sitting in a scarlet jumper.
I'll imagine what he's thinking.
He is picturing his alley
soon to fill with celebration
soon to fill with festive faces,
fill with masks and throwing plaster,
throwing of the chalky powder,
making ghosts out of the living,
throwing newspaper confetti
breaking with the daily labours.
He who mends the shoes will join them,
carnival means, stop the selling!
Shut up shop and leave the dwelling.
Meanwhile here he is the cobbler,
sat behind his ancient benching
having words with those who visit.
Sometimes it's about the weather;

mostly it's about the footwear,
helping those who tread in footwear
on and off the beaten pathways
in the many kinds of weather
in his mini thin moustaches.
Moccasins are not a problem.

Mike's muse, Luton versus Preston

Guardian Online report:

Last Saturday, Luton Town FC broke a losing streak after manager Mike Newell posted a copy of Kipling's 'If' in the dressing room. 'It is something that I have read for years,' he said. 'It's something I believe in and I have got it pinned up in my office. On Friday, I put it up in the dressing-room for some to read. I don't think many of the players could make head nor tail of it... I took it down before it could be defaced.'

The Town had played eight games and been defeated
      every time;
their manager Mike Newell thought, 'I'll fuel them
      with rhyme' –
the kind that stiffens sinews and goes rippling through
      the joints.
He chose Mr Kipling's poem 'If ', for picking up the
      points.

On the day before the fixture, he put up the rousing
      text
in the Kenilworth Road dressing room, the marvellous
      came next.

The players were bemused by this unorthodox
selection,
and bemusement is the key word here – the muse was
their infection:

A superhuman streak raced through the players as
they ran,
the goalie was as solid as an anchor, not a man.

Carlos Edwards got the second – he's from Trinidad
and Tobago,
and he made the Preston backs look like they suffered
from lumbago.

Yes, the players got the message, from what Rudyard
had penned.
Mr Newell found the fuel, and the iffyness would end.

Whipps Cross Hospital, 3rd January '45

Dear Glad,

I'm in the nurses' canteen, I've been nursing the men wounded in the air raid on the RAF base. And I've got to tell you, I've fallen for one of them. A little Frenchie he is. I've always liked the French: romantic, stylish and oniony. He says he wants to start a family and he says he wants to start it with me! He's been in England since all this started in '39 and he says he doesn't feel very French anymore, so I said when he's up and about, I'll take him down to Dover and we can look over at France. He says his mum used to dance on stage in Paris. Remember how we used to dance on the bandstand? I'll take him there and show him. He says if we get married, I'll have to become a Roman Catholic. I said, 'But you've only known me ten minutes. Seven, actually.' He said he knew I was the one for him in seven *seconds*. I said, 'What took you so long, I thought the French were supposed to be romantic.'

I miss you, Glad.
Your loving Sis

Donor poem

It should be widely heeded
that a flood of blood is needed
the balance in the banks
could be healthier, so thanks
to those who have the bottle
and those who let themselves be bleeded.

An anatomy of injury

My head was injured one day
when another boy found it to be just a stone's
     throw away
from his animosity.

My knee was injured one day,
when I fell onto the monstrosity of a splintered
     church organ
with a crash and a gash and a splash of crimson.

My forearm was cracked one Dunstable day
when I slipped off the slide and received a really nasty
     knock.

When I was knocked off my bicycle, I injured my
     testicle
and the policeman asked if I had received any injuries,
I said that I had not.

My heel was injured when I put my foot into the wheel
of my brother's motor-bicycle, rather than on the
     footrest.
We were unable to save the sock.

My pride was injured
when the teacher asked us who we thought
had come top of the class in the tests
and many said they thought it was me,
but it wasn't.
Then she asked who we thought
had come second
and many thought it was me,
but it wasn't.

I had come ninth.

*The Roman physician Galen with one
arm in plaster, ordering five pints*

Dear Sis,

I do miss you. If I ever get over to your side of the
world, I said to Bob, perhaps we could visit you there
in French Canada. The French can be so infuriating
but you've got to love them. I'm so in love with Joan
of Arc, even though she was against the English. On
a night out, me and Edie always used to head for the
Free French Club. It was her who discovered it. She
thought the French people there were romantic and
enchanting. So, it's funny I ended up with a Parisian
painter and she got a butcher from Southend.

Mind you Bob's not as French as he was... well he's
called Bob now, for a start. Everything's just gradually
got more English. We get one boy and we call him
René Marcel, eight years later another one comes along
and we call him John. There's still the odd French word
we use, though. When they pick their noses we tell
them not to play with their loos. I think it sounds less
common than bogies. Really I'd rather they didn't pick
their noses at all, but they're just kids aren't they, like
we were. Let's get our skates on and meet up, Glad.

As always,
Your sis

XXX

Ready for school and all ruffled,
wiping from my winter face
the kiss my mum had put in place, there.
And so I wore her heart
on my sleeve,
on the duffle-coated weaving.
Don't kiss me, Mum, I'd say.
And she'd say,
'Say PLEASE.'

Quackers

When we first moved from London, my father kept on his job in the capital. He would make his way each evening from High Holborn to St Pancras and then onwards by steam train, back to family and foodstuff.

He goes his way home through the early winter city, stopping to do brief business with a street vendor at a novelty stall, displaying a colourful variety of plastic frivolities. It's nearing Christmas. He'll get something for the youngsters. Some small, near-Christmas knick-knacks. The plastic ducks look good. The vendor demonstrates that they are whistles. Doubly good, then. Heading for the terminus, the train, and the *Evening News*, and the eventual warm embrace and nibble of a kiss.

Back in the home, my mother is well pleased with the bird presentation. My younger sister holds one and I the other. My older brother is above this brittle birdlife. Angela and I blow into the mouthpieces at the same moment. The bottom beak of each bird drops in slow response, and the quacking comes comically forth. 'They'll look nice on the tree,' Mum advises. Thread is found, along with their new hanging positions.

And henceforward, they come out annually to beduck the pineful foliage. The whistling ducks, ornamental now, are whistling ducks no longer. Seen. Not heard.

But there are worse endings at Christmas for a bird.

The last Skimpot Flyer

Skimpot is an area of Luton through which once ran a rail connection to London. The final service set out in April 1965 and a cluster of enthusiasts gathered to mourn and to moan and to celebrate. One of them considers.

Hatfield to Dunstable, no service, Constable.
What have they undone,
oh, what have they donestable?
Railing, not rolling, the whole thing is criminal.
Hatfield to Dunstable, something so beautiful.
What is the aftermath?
All that remains of the train is a photograph.
Locos so valiant, making the gradient,
ghost trains are all that remains of radiant.
People would often go walking to Totternhoe
once they had got to the Dunstable down-line,
then back on the up-line, a very slight incline
to Hatfield, or even the Capital Town.
And there was the firm which made stuff for the
    hatting trade,
they were so chuffed for they had their own branch,
worming away from the ranch of the factory,
that branch no more of it. Just like the rest of it,
cut down to none of it, that is the size of it.

One of the stations, I can't recall which one,
to get to it, you had a muddy old hike
and passengers left their galoshes 'til evening
in rows in the waiting room, waiting to greet all the
    feet of their owners
yes, you could just leave them, as safe as you like.
This little erosion, careering corrosion
of what was a thing of considerable class.
Not right to retire, that last Skimpot Flyer,
I'm glad I saluted, as it tootled past.

Train drawn by A. J. Curtis in the guise of Nigel

Extravagance

When I was a boy
extravagantly was not the way
things were done in our home.
Budgets and belts were tight.
Christmas, we pushed out the boat,
but measuredly:
one box of dates,
one packet of figs,
one bottle each of sherry and port.
As much as could be afforded.
And the lifting smoke of my father's cigar
was the star prize.
The smoke, he blew it upwards in a ring.
And he sat back with the comfort of a King
Edward.

Taking out the 'in it' and putting 'innit' in it

This clock has still got a lot of mileage in it.
This clock is well-stocked with mileage, innit.

This society has still got deep class divisions in it.
Classwise, this society is still deeply divided, innit.

This potato has the possibility of the most delightful
     bloom in it.
This potato is bloomful of possible delight, innit.

This gap between the floorboards has got some little
     bits of old cheese in it.
Have you thought about doing some hoovering, innit.

On the 9.30 to Newcastle

From a Canadian literary magazine,*
on our way to do a poetry show,
I read aloud, to Michael, the following.

'Like the Wooden Horse of Troy,
the poem is a gift
which contains something
hidden and a portent.'

And Michael says,
'Did you know PLUTONIUM
contains the word
LUTON?'

*Exquisite Corpse   Poet running for 9.30 to Newcastle

A show for my sister

When the cardboard curtain
came up to show
my first puppet performance,
it was for you and you only
my Space-hopping poppet.
You, in our living room
giving room to the scissor-snipped crew,
shipped in from Woolworths for a shilling.
My cut-out cast were not cut out
for anyone but you,
Angie Boo.
You, my key and only witness.
How willingly you paid your heed
and your entrance monies.
How eager your attention,
as each figure drew forth
the cutlass of its character
and spilled the beans of what it had to do.
What an audience you were, until you began fidgeting
in Act Twelve, Scene Two.

Postage stamps

I survey the pages of the hinged collection
once my father's,
now my own.
Every few years, I will inspect the perforated ranks
but only today do I understand,
only today do I truly receive my father's gift.
The Penny Black has just dropped
and I give thanks.
Now, I see my grandmother's tongue
applying moisture to the glue, throughout the ages
and my heart is all a-flutter
at these paper butterflies.
A shame we kept the stamps
and threw away the letters.

My dear grandchild,

Here in Nice it is a beautiful morning. Carnival time
has come round. Another winter so quick on the
heels of the last. My friend, Mireille, and I, have been
swimming in the sea, which buoys up the old body as
readily as the young.

Your Aunt Daisy and I have made our carnival masks
from papier-mâché.

They are next to the fire, drying on the dog.

Daisy has just asked me to place some of the carnival
confetti she has cut up into the envelope, so you can
share the spirit of the carnival when you throw it over
your own dog.

I sit here with the windows and shutters open.
Yes, here in Nice it is a beautiful morning and yet I
am desolate to hear of your terrible experience at the
school. Please make sure I have got the sequence of
events correct, because I am making correspondence
on your behalf.

So, you joined the Scottish Country Dancing class
in your lunch break. It was your first time and it

had taken courage to go along because some foolish boys see dancing as an activity to be ashamed of. After a while in the class, you nervously laughed out aloud because, for the first time, your feet were learning, learning the wonders of making dance steps. Intimidated by your laughter, the teacher ordered you out of the room, accusing you of play-acting and buffoonery.

This is the story as I understand it. Please hand the enclosed letter to the woman, along with the photograph of myself on stage with the most famous dancing company in all of France. I want her to realise the calibre of dancing stock with which she is toying. As a dancer in Paris I would kick my legs and laugh, laugh, laugh. Laugh at the filth who came to ogle us from the pit. Except your grandfather of course.

Your grandmother

More Angie Boo

When I sang my song about the bungalow in Luton
and I said that my father cleared the snow
making a line to mark the neighbour's bit of pavement
over which he wouldn't go,
my sister told me that this did not ring true.
She reminded me
that when a bungalow resident left their washing
    on the line
with the weather, nice and fine
and then went out to the shops, say,
when the rains came,
a neighbour would come
and take the laundry off the line
and into their own dwelling for you.
An act of telling camaraderie
indicated Angie,
Angie who once upon a time
would sit in the grate
scoffing coal out of the scuttle,
like it was chocolate.
Dad used to tell us, 'Use a plate'
but not in such an instance.

And Angie took the goldfish from their chilly little
    bowl and softly stroked them.
She didn't get the difference
between the different kinds of pet.
Yet, now she is a different kind of Angie:
fossil fuel she never eats
although occasionally she does present her family
with the odd dead fish or two.
Angie Boo.

French Grandma visits English bungalow

As a result of living in America, Dad would sometimes refer to himself as Pop. His mother dropped by the bungalow just once in the 1960s.

Grandma arrives while Dad's at work.
She is sat with Mum, myself and my sister.
Dad lets himself in. The dog barks.
Dad comes through to the living room.
They clasp eyes, they clasp bodies, they step back
and the rasping talk begins.
A surging fury of spectacular speaking,
sparking, blazing, amazing
crazed cackle
of the two
locked
back,
clocked
into shattering unity.
Shocking, knocking on twenty years since they last
    cast eyes
upon the eyes and the size of each other.
A right old trembling tear-drop tumbling ensues.

Embracing, facing this deliverance from near-on two
        decades of out-of-touching
hanky-drenched, the French is freed.
The frog in the throat croaks again.
Dad's secret identity is rumbled. Mother and child
        united.
Child and mother-tongue, united.
To Luton from Nice, to release the unspoken.
A voice broken for the second time
and climbing to the top.
Snap
Cackle
and Pop.

Mental

I recently contributed to a forum on 'The Stigma of Mental Illness'. Shortly before the event I was at a girl's school in St Albans and attempted to broach the subject with the teenagers.

I mentioned to the students, a character in my work who had a violent aversion to any sort of furniture. Any chair, table or wardrobe, freestanding or fitted. We agreed that he had a Compulsive Obsessive Disorder. I asked the children to describe characters with aversions and compulsions of their own. One of them invented a girl who did not like clocks because they always told her she was late. A strong example of evading the problem by focusing on an effect rather than a cause.

We discussed various conditions and syndromes and it felt that our discourse was increasing understanding and tolerance. One youngster said she knew a person who had Tourette's syndrome, someone who would constantly scream out loud for no reason. She said it was the Headmistress.

When I was a schoolchild of nine or ten, there was a man called Bill, who we called Car-Driver Bill, because

he would sit on the wall opposite the school gates
going through the motions of driving an invisible car.
I would always ensure that I passed him on the
opposite side of the street, without making eye contact.
When my French grandmother visited us, she came
up to the school to pick me up and because she was
a woman of curiosity, on seeing Bill in action, she
recommended we go over and ask him for a lift.
Hearing her French accent, Bill said 'Please climb in,
Madame. There's not a lot of room in these MGBGTs,
not even this 3.5 litre model, so it'll be a bit of a squeeze
for one of you in the back, I'm afraid.'

Twenty-five years later, I am in London, going for a job
with a theatre company. The director happens to ask
where I was educated. When I mention my primary
school, she tells me that her husband's uncle has lived
opposite this school all his life. She says that he likes
to sit on his outer wall going through the motions of
driving an imaginary vehicle. I say, 'Is his name Bill?'
and she says, 'Yes it is.' I say, 'Is he still driving the
MGBGT?' and she says, 'No, he drives a truck now, he's
just got his HGV licence.'

My dearest grandchild,

It was the greatest pleasure for me to finally come from France to visit you in your home in the English town of Luton and to sit with you and your sister and make masks. The paints which I brought with me, came from the very shop in Nice which provided materials for the French genius of Henri Matisse. So, of course, I had to take them home with me. Henri was the name of your grandfather, my husband. His mother was French as were both of my own parents, so you have three French grandparents and yet your father has not taught you a word of the language.

I also saw that your father has made not one new painting in England. In the 1930s when we returned from the United States, his whole weekends were spent depicting exactly the old town of Nice. He was not a Braque. He was not even a Picasso. I sensed he painted to reclaim his country after seven years of absence. To secure his heritage. To anchor his being. This was the work of his art. It is possible that art can challenge, question, re-evaluate, make money. Your father's art did none of these, but still he had talent, and if he had persevered he might have been able to support his poor mother whose only pillow is her dog,

Your poor grandmother

Sooty, or the bird that reminded me of my French Grandma

It must have come sweeping down the bungalow
        chimney
when the fire was off duty
that feathery black beauty
that was never going back up the smokestack.
Was it a crow?
Was it a raven?
Or was it a very sooty pigeon?
We didn't know.
We just knew that whatever it was,
it didn't want to go.
For all our shuffling and shooing,
nothing doing, going-wise.
That ruffled kerfuffle,
flitting around the sitting room
eventually sitting down at rest
on the central light fitting.
Eyeing us.
Contemplating starting up a nest, perhaps.
So I run to the bungalow's rear
splaying open the French windows.
The bird follows and flies
steering away through the stretching gap

going back to its element
and my mum begins to clap
that ruffled kerfuffle
that disorderly duster,
that freaky beaky bungalow invader,
that got us in a right flap.

My dear grandchild,

Thank you for the drawing of your dog which is accurate but lacking in vitality. I can see that the creature is asleep, like our own, here beside the fire. It is a challenge to breathe life into the image. A challenge to which you have failed to rise. If I did not tell you such things, I would be shirking my work as a grandmother.

So, you wish for an old woman's advice about approaching this young beauty at your school. My advice is plain. If you love her, tell her. I cannot make it plainer. If you love her. Tell her. Spill the beans, as your grandfather would say. It did not continue between him and I, but still I will love him for all of my days.

He called me his Blancmange. I called him my Potato, because he was versatile and his collars were very well starched. In French, we say *tu me manques*: you are missing to me. The beloved is put first and not the self. Put the beloved first. Write to this girl of your feelings. Let the beans be spilled. But do not bother to enclose any of your drawings.

Your grandmother

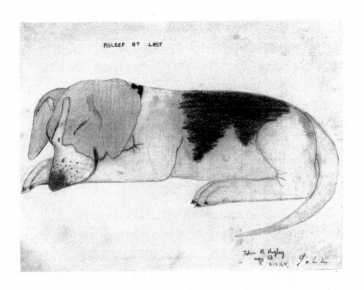

ASLEEP AT LAST

John R Hughes
age 13
2.1.64.

At the pictures

He's standing in a cinema in Mysore
it's the last day of a lengthy working life.
He's the longest-serving usher
on this side of all Russia
and he's never had promotion or a wife.

He's just sat out his last romantic fable.
Now, he's standing at a sandwich-laden table
he's organised himself a leaving do,
he didn't expect many, but there isn't even anybody
let alone a couple or a few.

It isn't that the usher isn't popular,
it's just the way things sometimes will conspire,
the other usher's mother had an illness.
The ticket seller's sister had a fire.

Way back in the middle of the sixties
the usher had a romance of his own,
the girl who sold the ice creams
warmed the usher to the bone.
And he hoped they would be wedded

but confetti wasn't shredded
and no rice grains got depacketed or thrown.

It wasn't that she didn't like his manner.
She loved the way he swung his torch about.
She would blush beside the usher
but her father, he would hush her,
'You're not wedding him while I'm alive' he'd shout.

In the seventies this usher very nearly got promotion
when the manager went off to Bangalore,
but some monies were backhanded
and it left the usher stranded
and the prospects of promotion were no more.

In the eighties and the nineties, not much happened,
the cinema continuing to fill.
But the films weren't to his liking, like the old days.
The millennium went by without a thrill.

Today's the day he goes into retirement
all on his own, he's laid out all the spread,
the boss he didn't mind
although he couldn't stay behind
as he had other stuff he had to do instead.

The usher is about to put the sandwiches away,
shut up shop and put the keys in through the letterbox,
when shock of shocks

who is it comes a-swinging through the door?
Yes, it's the one who sold the ice creams in the sixties,
not the character who left for Bangalore. (Who he also
    invited).

'Anouk, Anouk,' says the usher
'Mukesh, my special one,' replies the guest.
'My father has relented
and a wedding dress I've rented
and India have won the Second Test.'

Sent

There were the paintings done by Dad.
There was the brass done by Mum.
There was the fencing trophy won by my brother.
There was my Subbuteo out in the other room
and, there was Angela's Spacehopper,
full of puff, in the garden.

There were those solid, pink, scented sweets Grandma
used to send us, I just don't think
they suited the English palate.

That's why in the bungalow, they always went into
the bin.

And there were those kids playing football on the
green outside the home.
They drove Mum up the wall.

We left because of that football on the green.
Because of the wall Mum had been driven up.
Mel says we should have gone out to those kids
and given them the sweets that Grandma sent.

Osmosis – no

I'm seventeen, I've moved to Bristol
I don't like the relocation
I'm not gregarious at all.
It is appalling isolation.
I do A-Level Biology
we are told of the osmotic
yes, I get it Mr Wagner, but I haven't really got it.
There is no osmosis.
In terms of something happening, I'd say there's
    nothing doing
there's no fro and there's no to-ing
there's no mutual imbuing.
There is no osmosis.
Osmosis is when water moves from one cell to another
when the level falls in one, and then it rises in the other
'til the water level's level, in the two adjacent bodies:
it may take two to tango but I only know what odd is.
There is no osmosis. I don't have the process.
I'm so inessential.
There's no water potential.
The lack of what is coming through, is torrential.
    There is no osmosis.

No man is an island but this adolescent might be
if I'm taking it from anyone, I take it very lightly
the lack of to and froing, it is going on for stunning,
like a pair of Shetland Islands where the ferry isn't
    running:
there is no osmosis
and there's no symbiosis,
but that's another story.

Another one for Eve to mark out of 10 on a Post-it note

I can see myself at seventeen,
we've relocated down to Bristol.
My new school is not my scene
and what I've got to do is crystal-clear to me.

So I go to the school deputy, the deputy headmaster:
'Mr Sculthorpe, I am off to get a job, I've got to go.'
He smiles and says 'Stay on a while,
at least secure a job before you go.'
But I want to go much faster
and I say, 'No.'
He'd prefer, 'No Sir' but doesn't say.
I'm seventeen and stupid and I get on my way.

But, I cannot get a job although I try and try,
I feel it's a disaster and I cry and cry,
'Dad, will you stop trying to console me!'
Then I decide to stuff my pride,
I'll go to Mr Sculthorpe and I'll see if he'll agree to
    re-enrol me.

Knocking on his door, I'm sure I'll be as welcome as a
    rat.

But he makes me feel I'm wanted:
I'm seventeen and stupid, he knows that.
'We're here to teach you.
We're here to reach you,
even though you're seventeen and stupid.'
But now I am no longer in that state.
Now I'm stupid and I'm fifty-eight.

A. J. Curtis and the fish

I walk with Tony.
Moonshine big, a bright and Brighton button
        overhead.
We tread the homeward esplanade.
The scaly plateful those unruly waves have laid
        before us
is now tight in Tony's wide
and grateful grasp:
this tossed marine inhabitant,
windfallen fruit of the sea.

Three years before, the world had thrown up Tony.
It was back in Bristol. We the energetic students
set about the brightening of our gloomy 6th Form
        Common Room.

Tony, in the year below me, was unknown to me.
He had dipped his bare feet in the paint bucket.
And we held him bodily, topside down
and he walked the planks of strutted ceiling,
making all his markings there
and mightier impression on me.

My mate to be: in a world of pranks and
    disappointments,
an Artist.
And now,
here he is beside this sea, with the gift of fish
in his fingers.

Just for a chuckle, Tony once hurled his crash helmet
arcing into the surging waters of Vassals Park.

And now, out of the dark, the world has thrown him
    back
a mackerel.

Dear Glad,

Bristol is the right place. It's been an upheaval, alright.
Marcel won't leave the airport to join us, but he has to
make his own choices. We all do.

I'm sorry to take John away from his friends and his
football but he's got a good school. The new youngsters
will take a bit of getting used to. They do speak odd
here. We have a bit of fun imitating them. Not in a
nasty way, though. Angela's fine. She's such a lovely
girl. My precious.

It's very icy here at the moment. Please get your skates
on and come see us. Canada's had more than its fair
share of you. It's been great to start work again and
hand over the hovering to Bob. Hoovering, I mean.
He's got the gardens lovely, as usual, front and back,
and he's started painting gnomes that a neighbour
over the road first moulds in concrete. It's great for him
to be painting again and you can't do landscapes all
your life. Well, you can, but I'm not going to spoil it for
him. He loves sitting out in the shed, giving them their
own colours and characters. He's started giving them
names, but I said you don't want to bother if you're not
going to keep them. They're such cheerful little chaps.

He's been taking them round the village trying to make some sales. He's sold four already, three of them to me.

You're missed, Sis
Your sis

New home with
Huw Gnome

Borrowing the brother-in-law's wheelbarrow

Today my brother-in-law lent me
    his wheelbarrow.
He said that although he is no churchgoer
he does have sympathy with what the believer
    is trying to do
in terms of treating others as they would be treated
    themselves.
As a mark of solidarity, he WOULD
lend me his wheelbarrow.
Yes, had he been wheelbarrowless, he said,
he would like to think that somebody
would be willing to lend him theirs.
The difference being, of course, that he,
would not have the audacity
to ask.

Straightening a record

'We had no exposure to uncles or aunts
my dad's only friends were his God and his plants.'
As I read this aloud from the page of my book
on stage at the Leeds City Varieties
I felt the need to vary.
For my lines were contrary to the truth.
'My dad's only friends were his God and his plants
... and The Petleys,' I added.
And I'd swear I heard a grateful sigh
from somewhere in that Yorkshire night
as I put to right that easy lie,
doing justice to that other mum and dad
so loved by my own
whom Mum and Dad, in turn, were loved by:
David and Freda Petley.
When David was courting Freda, he came to pick
her up, with his car heated up, by a brick.
And the two of them warmed my Mum and Dad
    through to the quick.
To the soul.
To the gearstick.

Keeping Mummy

Mummy, when I cut my chin
you came and kept the bleeding in
you clasped it like it was a purse
way back once, you were a nurse.
You shone my brother's fencing trophy on the
    mantle-shelf
and you ensured my sister felt of value, when unsure
    of it herself.
You strenuously stretched the pound,
you even found enough for me to visit distant Fourth
    Division football grounds,
like Chesterfield and Barrow.
You darned the socks, you knitted too,
for me you recommended blue.
While we still had the stairs to tread
you held me very tightly when you took me nightly
    up to bed.
You knitted up my broken skin,
this narrow mark upon my chin's
a mark
of how you held it all together, Mum.
Our Daddy's wage was not a hoard

but you ensured
we always had the best you could afford.

In nineteen-seventy, we come
to Bristol City, 'cos my mum
has seen an advert for some rows
of brand new chalet bungalows,
at knockdown prices in The West
and Mum knows bungalows the best.
My dad has just retired from work,
but not a man to rest or shirk
he takes up all the household chores.
He does the carpet on all fours.
He empties bins, he fills the shelves
while Mum, the younger of themselves
she gets a Mini, eight years old,
she gets a man to paint it gold.
And once a week her hair is dressed
inside the chalet in The West
and once a month she takes the test
to lose the pesky Learner's plate.
It takes a while, it's worth the wait.
And Gladys comes to add to this
from Canada, to see her sis
and this completes my mother's bliss.
So many years since they last clapped
their eyes and hands and overlapped.
And Glad goes home and when she's gone,

my mum she drives the motor on.
The key is curled, the world ignites.
She drives and Dad, he dips the lights.

You held the wheel.
You held me tight.
You kept our dwellings bright and clean
and though our daddy's earnings were not large,
you ensured we always had
the best
of margarine.

Dear Grandchild,

Thank you for the drawing of the home you have left behind. Of course you will miss your brother. He has remained in Luton because his destiny is there. Unfortunately this is of no comfort.

Now that you have left this town, and you are in the countryside, I look forward to the impressions of the trees and tributaries. They will go up on my wall and call to me. They will call to me from you. From your heart, from Pucklechurch.

Please make sure you always draw with your heart. Otherwise the pictures will be of no use to me. I do not ask for accuracy, I am not a town planner. I am your grandmother. And I send you real French kisses.

Your grandmother

Dear Grandma,

I have written some stories of my own about a
mysterious Frenchman called Monsieur Robinet. It is
a way of me taking hold of the mysterious French part
of my family that is you, and Dad a bit. I am trying to
shed light upon the side of my moon that was hidden,
all except for that one wonderful afternoon of you and
Dad showing and shining. But how soon that balloon
was gone. It is part of my defining. Mum changed her
name from Ivy to Jeanne because of Jeanne d'Arc.
Mum thought that brave young fighter was the real
thing. A French drenching of heroism. But then Mum
changed again to Joan. Because Jeanne was a bit
too much. Mum thinks you are the real thing too,
Grandma – but sometimes the real thing is a bit too
much.

Keep in touch,
Your loving grandsuch

R.Hagley 193
VIEUX NICE
Traced by J. Hagley_with added H.Robinet

92

Aurangzeb and his dad

Delhi. 1658. Shah Jahan has been imprisoned by his son who has taken over the running of the country. Aurangzeb's rule is very very strict. But he relaxes the ferocity of his regime, by allowing his father to remain alive.

Aurangzeb: Father, I bring you sweets.

Shah Jahan: You bring me bitterness.

Aurangzeb: It is necessary for our country to have strong leadership.

Shah Jahan: You think me weak? And yet, not so weak that you will allow me my freedom. You announce that you wish to uphold the traditions of our nation and yet you treat your king and your father like a dog.

Aurangzeb: Look, do you want these sweets or what?

Alternatives to losing your temper

Sit on your hands.
Visit the Hebrides.
Knit. Unknit your brow.
Build a model of your anger out of matches.
Catch a falling star and put it in a poem.
Watch a soap.
Make some soap.
Send the world a message of hope.
Coil up in a medicine ball.
Call a nurse.
Reverse.
Close your eyes and do the washing up.
Sing.
Pray.
Have a fig roll.
Have a nice day.

PEACE

Delighting the Daleks

In the Gloucestershire classroom
we did a Dalek drawing workshop
I wanted to get each girl and boy
to give their Dalek something
to increase the peace
and decrease the desire to destroy.
To spread a bit of Dalek joyfulness.
A few of the children gave their creature a friend,
one was given a bath,
another was given some toast
and one of the Daleks got pregnant.

Out on the buses

A piece appeared in the Guardian *told by one of two West Country busmen whose love for each other was not appreciated by all. There follows an effort to retell this man's story in verse, as he remembers his John.*

John, he was a driver on the Seventy-eight,
I was on the One-o-three.
Me, I had always looked pretty straight,
he was more Freddie Mercury.
And he
was the man for me
and we were the talk of the depot,
down in Torquay.

Down at the depot, we used to smile
and stop for a chat,
but it was only a little while
before we knew it would be much more than that,
the place we were driving at
where we'd both wear the trousers, and the driver's hat.

On the edge of the morning,
he's out in the kitchen cooking.
The day is still yawning
and we've already let love get a look in.

He gave me a silvery cigarette lighter,
it was brighter than the others,
it was a Zippo.
Hold on tight
for heaven's light
when his sickness really began to bite
and he had to leave the depot,
he was still nosey
about the bus Stasi.
I kept him in touch with which inspector said what to
        such and such,
I kept him in touch.
He'd never hold another steering wheel
and I held him in my arms
and I told him I loved him very much.
You've got to let a little love get a look in.

On the edge of his hospital bed
the linen's as white as any swan.
I went out for a cigarette
I came back in and he was gone.
Sometimes us chaps, we had to keep our love under
        wraps,
and now here's a little rhapsody for John, Bohemian
        John.

The things that people used to say
when they found out we were
from Torbay.

Dad bus chat 1973

Dad: I'm very proud of you working on the bus, John. When I got on, I thought – I know that conductor...

Me: I always wanted to be a bus conductor, and now at 19, I am one – do you think I've peaked a bit too early?

Dad: You loved that conductor's uniform you had for Christmas, didn't you?

Me: It's a shame you couldn't respect the uniform and refrain from hitting me.

Dad: It's not something I'm proud of. You wanted to get me angry and you managed it marvellously. It was poor parenting on my part.

Me: You encouraged me in my art and my writings and my music – not in my dancing, mind – but I always felt you were on my side – I just should have learned to dodge the punches.

Dad: I never punched you!

Me: I know you never, Dad – and with this ticket

machine I only get to wind out the tickets,
I never get to punch them, like I did that
Christmas.

Dad: Yes, I thought, when I got on... I know that
conductor.

Me: But *do* you know me, Dad?

Dad: I know I love you.

Me: That'll do. Now tell me something. Did Mum
get on with Grandma?

Dad: She was a very strong personality.

John : Who was?

Dad: Exactly. It was a bit difficult.

John: So, why did you stop?

Dad: Stop what?

John: Painting.

Dad: I stopped painting because I had you lot.
The art wasn't needed,
it was secondary.
It had had its day.
When art becomes secondary, put it away.
And I wasn't that good, anyway.

John: Good enough for me.

Dad: Thank you.

100

Dear Dad,

Here is my picture of you watching the telly with your sunglasses on.

Your neat garden is in the background. And you are dreaming that the gnomes are saints. The ones that you newly painted this morning, this is. That are not in the picture, except inside your bonce.

I do regret your not getting to teach me your mother language, and I do regret us never hanging about together in your motherland, but it's a tiny pebble of regret in the happy heap of what you and Mum had.

There are two photos of the two of you, some twenty-five years between. In both, your arm is keen around Mum's shoulder. In the one where you are older, it is around her just that little bit tighter.

You didn't speak French to us, but you told Mum over and over that you loved her making your dinner and you loved her bringing the light and soul and the party to your existence when you had for a time, thought that true happiness was a lie,

and you loved her, so.

Love John

P.S. What do you think of my drawing?

The bus is more us with a crew

Driver: You ought to think about learning to drive. This route will be OMO in a few years.

Conductor (John): What's OMO?

Driver: One Moron Operated.

Conductor: Not Oxy Moron Operated?

Driver: That's right.

Conductor: I'm not going to stay on the buses, I'm going to Uni.

Driver: What's that? University is it? What, Bristol University?

Conductor: No. I want to go up North, I go to Bradford.

Driver: Will you miss us?

Conductor: I'll miss playing cribbage in the canteen and helping the elderly and the infirm on and off the vehicle, in my uniform.

Driver: The drivers won't be able to do that, of course.

Conductor: I know. This OMO lark won't improve things... how come they're allowed to make unnecessary changes that make matters worse?

Driver: Maybe you'll find out at university.

Conductor: I won't – I'm studying Sociology.

Medusa, the loser

I'm the head that he cut off
and he carries me in a bag.
He drags me out
to wave about
if ever there's an enemy
he wants to turn to stone.
He uses me.
I want my bleeding body back
so I can feel, at least
that I am *totally* alone.

Do sneak in a snake of your own

Woolly snake

Mum: I'm going to miss you when you're up at
         university, John.

John: I'll come home every holiday.

Mum: Good boy... I want you to take this woollen
         snake with you as a mascot.

John: Bradford is famous for its wool, Mum.

Mum: Well, you're taking it to the right place, then.

John: I'll write to you and tell you about it.

Mum: Good boy.

John: It's a door-stop as well isn't it?

Mum: A draft-excluder you mean – it's cold up there.
         Drafty.

John: It's very thoughtful of you.

Mum: You're my child.

John: Every time the wind tries to come under my
         door, Mum, I'll think of you giving me this
         snake.

Mum: Make sure you do.

The woollen horse of Halifax

It was up in hilly Halifax
at holly time of year,
Polly was in pantomime,
she played the horse's rear.
Her shimmy was a triumph
and up the front was Jimmy,
what a dear.
He'd neigh
in such a cheerful way
while Polly did her walk,
the wonder-horse of Halifax
became the season's talk,
they came from Leeds and Barnsley,
but they didn't come from York.
Or Harrogate.

When the pantomime
had done its time
the two remained a pair,
deciding that their lives were now
the thing that they would share.
The costume where the two had met
in due course was released

by the Halifax theatre
and for one final performance, the two became
    the beast.
And at their wedding in the chapel, the priest
having blessed them with a smile,
went riding on the bride and groom,
went giddy, up the aisle.

I like some English Panto fun
And I like Morris tunes
But I don't like it overdone
Like I don't like my prunes.

Morris

The Morris once, was for the man
but now the other gender can
engender its own style.
The Morris, it is versatile.
I've seen the stick and bell and cloth
appropriated by the Goth.
The Morris it may go to seed,
but flower again it shall indeed
and powerfully blossom out
as hearty as a Brussels sprout.

With the Morris Men of Hammersmith
I danced out in The Square.
With all ages of citizen, I quickly learned to share
the step and flick of handkering, required for the
    parade.
In and out of local shops
and in and out of shade,
as the concertina played
and assistants weren't resistant,
though no purchases were made.

It doesn't help, it may be said
the way we don't promote the tread
of Morris manners in the school,
they've hardly heard of Squire and Fool.
I took some inner-city youth to meet the Bampton
    Squire,
he taught them but the basics, but I tell you, they
    caught fire.
The little with which they were hit, set city eyes alight.
'This is alright,' said one '... This Morrisons Dancing.'

Stick and hanky, step and line
there's rumours that it's in decline.
My answer is a little dull:
there's no decline, it's just a lull.
Like concertinas squeezed to shut
until the arms unbend,
like deckchairs go back in the hut
at every summer's end – but out again that seating
    comes,
like dentures in and out of gums.

A tried and tested treasure, sure;
the Morris, Doris, shall endure.

Maurice
(dancing)

At a public reading by an English hero

Tell us about Copperfield and Oliver
and his wishing for the dishing out of more
let's hear about the optimist Micawber,
his persistent hopes of what lay up afore.
Do divulge of Mister Scrooge and poor
    Miss Havisham,
that disenchanted woman who set all her world
    alight.
Tell us any of your stories that you fancy
but please don't tell us Nancy's tale tonight.

Let your prose expose those social conditions
where there should be an improvement of the plight.
Tell us and impel us to correction,
to protection and to setting things aright.
Perhaps pick one of Mister Pickwick's Papers,
Dingley Dell at Christmastime, would do us very well
but please don't tell us Nancy's tale tonight.

Don't spill the beans of her and Bill.
Don't put your public through the mill,
Mr Dickens as you will
yes, as you fancy, up until

That villainous and sinking bag of spite.
Let common sympathy prevail
leave us hearty, leave us hale
and please don't tell us Nancy's tale tonight.

Dear Mister Pickwick,

I have been reading your papers, and am enjoying
your capering very much. I obtained my green volume
of these adventures from my local public library
lending department. I feel sure that your creator,
Mister C. Dickens, would have approved of such places
– particularly because of the benefit to readers unable
to afford a text of their own. I have renewed the book
4 times and paid about 70 pence in fines, but you are
worth it. 70 pence is fourteen shillings in your money.
There have been many changes since your day; far
fewer people wear hats for instance. Also, in your day,
did you have, I wonder, telescopic handles to pull your
luggage along? You are always travelling about, aren't
you? Today, I read aloud a bit of one of your travels to
some blue-clad schoolchildren in Northumberland
– the story where you mistakenly settled in the twin
room of a hotel in Ipswich, which was actually the
accommodation of an unsuspecting woman. There
you were, in your nightcap, behind the curtain of the
bed, ready for sleeping when in she comes and starts
her preparations for dreaming, not dreaming that you
are in the immediate vicinity. I asked the youngsters
to relate the tale in verse and one of them put: 'Mister

Pickwick went to bed, with his nightcap on his head.'
(Yes, you even wore hats to sleep in in your day.) And
someone else called Shannon wrote, 'Mr Pickwick in
his night cap, watching the woman take off her slap.'
Yes, Mister Pickwick, you can be gratified in knowing
that the youth of another millennium are engaged by
your appearance, your ambience and your antics. Here
is a drawing for you to complete.

Your admirer

A chat not far from Stamford Hill

A conversation between myself and Mr John Keats, in which I have a show to perform, in the town of Stamford, where there will be shown a tale of himself on film.

John, me   John, I'm off to Stamford Flat.

John Keats Where's that?

John, me   It's Lincolnshire and Rutland way.

J.K.   On the level?

J.   I'd say so – it's Fenland!

J.K.   Well, I'll be there, this Sunday actually, my *Bright Star* film is on the screen.

J.   On the level?

J.K.   Yes, unless someone in the cinema pushes out the cloth so that the projection is all lumpen with their form.

J.   I'll be there, just the day after. Will you be able to stay on for a little…

J.K.   Laughter?

J.   Yes.

J.K.   No, I'll be gone, John.

J.   Can't you stay, a tiny bit, in Stamford Flat, before you flit?

J.K.   My train is booked and I must quit. *It's an advance purchase ticket!* The cost would be ten pounds to change it. *TEN POUNDS!*

Keep your receipts, Mister Keats

A song composed whilst researching John Keats with an
imminent visit to The Marine Theatre in Lyme, home of
local heroine Mary Anning, famous for her fossil-hunting

I'm going to Lyme Regis, is it Dorset, is it Devon,
       soon I'll know.
I've been told there was a fossil-finding woman of
       Lyme Regis, long ago.
She sold her finds as curios.
She sounds to be somebody most intriguing
but my curiosity's directed elsewhere at the mo.
I've been going through the poetry and letters
of a man who didn't have sufficient time.
A man who walked on Hampstead Heath in autumn
with his vessel full of Mister William Shakespeare and
       the fruitfulness of rhyme.

John Keats, with your days laid out so meagre,
it is no surprise
how eager was your pace.
John Keats, you stuffed your notebook, rather than
       your ego and your face.

John Keats, you sat outside on coaches
it encroached upon your health,

your wealth did not provide the funds
for you to settle in the dry
you'd have preferred.
John Keats, you did the doctor's training
but decided you were cut out for the word.

The first I heard you mentioned was in a Loudon
     Wainwright song
then, in a another one by Morrissey
I didn't know your legacy,
but, still I sang along.

I've been going through the poetry and letters
of a man who later than his life
was so much better known.
A man whose pay day came too late for him to get a
     ticket
to get sat inside the coach
instead of getting wet and windblown.
Up beside the driver,
a man who was no skiver.
But the world it can deprive a
man, no matter what his feats.
Can I lend you a fiver, please?
No, make that a tenner, Sweet
John Keats.

John Keats, you wanted to complete a life that was held
    completely in the grip of poetry, because poetry
    you held to be most naturally holy.
John Keats, you suggested that a poem should come
    out complete,
as certain and as surely as a leaf upon a tree,
but preferably,
not as slowly.

Did you used to walk the dog?
Did you have a dialogue?
While the dog did what it had to do
did you share a verse or two
And were they the doggie's treats?
Poetry's apostle:
he's gonna be collosal.
He's not some kind of fossil,
young John Keats.

To Mr. John Keats 31 . i . 12
On the 73 bus (Northbound)

Dear John

I've just been running a workshop
in Swiss Cottage, not far from where you
used to live. We performed your Grecian
Urn one. I told them that I hadn't realised
the poem was about what was painted on
the vase; so for ages I wondered what the
heaven you were on about. And then Andy
explained to me that the scene you described
was not <u>near</u> the vase but <u>part</u> of it
and the penny dropped about why nothing
and no one was moving. So I got the
students to each go and find an object
and then they did stuff to give us clues
about it, until the penny dropped and
someone could name the object and <u>one</u>
thing was described in <u>your</u> kind of lingo,
a throat spray bottle, I think it was;
I lost my concentration a bit. But it's
really nice that people studying in the
Central School of Speech and Drama are being
influenced by you. And I really like the phrase
in the poem "fair attitude", it's what we need more
of nowadays, urnestly yours, John

120

Dear John Keats,

Last Thursday, I was round your house in Hampstead
where I bought a book of letters you had written in
the early nineteen-hundreds. I was with Celia. It was
really a lovely afternoon and we took tea on your
verandah, on the bench.

And slugging on that mug of tea,
it would be unknown to me
that in my bag and in your book,
there you are John, slagging off the French
 manner of speaking.
It's my father's native country.
It's my father's mother's lingo!
You went into your toolbag and you went in with a
 spanner and a cheeky monkey-wrench,
when you were slagging off the language of
 the French.
Is 'slagging off', a turn of phrase you know, John?
Do you like DIY or Dan Defoe, John?
I'd like to meet you sometime and to have a good
 old natter.

Do you use powder on your teeth, are you
	a hatter on The Heath?
John, you may be miles away,
in spite of which, I'd like to say

John, *je suis si enchanté*,
'scuse my French

P.S. It's some days later and I realise it's not just the
French, is it, John? No, you are not too keen on the
people of Devon, either. One letter says the battle of
Waterloo would have been lost, were all Englishmen
Devonians. And then the Scots, you say they are
comparatively clean but they never laugh. I told this to
a Scottish friend, who said, 'That made me laugh, but
then, I've got some Irish in me.' Let's not go into what
you say about the Irish!

Kilburn, April 2012

Kilburn's famous for its Irish, but I speak of an event
when on the patron saint of England's day
up Kilburn way, I went.
It was the Tricycle Theatre in the furbished
      auditorium:
a Monday morning on St George's Day.
There were maybe eighty teenagers, from countries far
      from England,
many of them countries where it wasn't safe to stay.
The writers' association, English PEN, had paid my
      wage
to stand up for the students in Asylum, on the stage.
I asked if one such student would translate into their
      language
a verse of mine, as line by line I'd say it from the page.
And many of them called the name of one they
      thought most suited
but, I looked at him they singled out and me, I had my
      doubt
about the willingness of him to so engage.
I addressed his fellows sitting in the plush.
They continued with their calling out, I called on them
      to hush.

Some of you have come from countries
where there is fear and fighting.
My country here, has problems
but it offers some restraint.
And if this lad you've singled out
don't want to ride this Tricycle,
then in England, on Saint George's Day
up Kilburn way,
HE AIN'T GONNA.

It sounded like some dragon had got inside and
     enraged me,
but the lad said he was willing and to his fellows'
     thrilling
he came up
and most efficiently,
he totally upstaged me.

You can draw your own dragon (and fill in the scales on this one?)

Tupuna

I have a photo taken in Nice in 1936, depicting my
great grandma, my grandma and Aunt Didi, my dad's
sister. I have carried this image of those three French
women with me on occasions. It is a reminder of the
French fraction of my heritage.

Before making my last trip to New Zealand, I had been
reading up on 'Kiwi' words and phrases in a book
kindly sent by a journalist, who had read of my interest
in his country's lingo. Many of the words were of Maori
origin, a sign of the way the original culture is a part
of New Zealand life today. I noticed different words for
Family and for Wider Family. I wondered whether the
trio in my photograph would be called family, or wider
family, being as a great grandmother was present.
In the Dance and Drama College in Wellington,
I was invited to a traditional welcoming ceremony.
A Powhiri. I was to be welcomed, along with a
Canadian theatre company, called The Wardrobe.
It was explained to me that this welcome would be
managed by someone with some authority in the
community, who would invite us to speak. We were
then to greet, each of the welcoming committee, who

would stand in line behind the welcomer. One was to give to each of them the Maori 'Hongi' – the sharing, nose to nose, of breath and eye contact. The intimacy of welcome.

The students were gathered in the hall and I and the other guests, were beckoned. We sat, as the students performed the ritual Haka. A young man stepped forward and spoke in a language I assumed to be Maori. I was informed that he was the welcoming dignitary, the son of a Cook Island chief. As had been explained to me, the guests were then expected to respond.

I stood up and performed a poem, then the Canadians elected one of their number to make a speech. We were all then signalled to greet each of those in the line. With one after another, I shared breath and eye contact. At the end of the line, I turned, expecting to find the Canadians close behind me. But I had misunderstood the instruction: you did the Hongi, you then had a bit of chat. My own version was referred to as 'speed Hongi-ing'.

After the ceremony I spoke with the Chief's son. He asked about my background. I mentioned my French roots and showed him the photograph of my three French relations. I asked him if these would be referred to as Family or Wider Family. He asked me if they were gone. I said that they were. He told me that they were

my ancestors, My Tupuna. They are always with me.
He explained that the word Tupuna is derived from
Tu – stand, and Puna – stream. Our ancestors stand
behind us, as we face our future which approaches in
the stream of life. I might have asked how a deceased
mother, manages to stand behind a number of her
children at the same time, in a variety of locations,
but I didn't. I didn't need to, for the idea transcended
rationale and was sustained by its beauty.

Feel free to give the river some tiddlers

Worries and beauties

In Australia, it was 'No worries'. In New Zealand, 'It's beautiful'. When I came back from the Antipodes, I tried to incorporate the two ideas into my life: It's beautiful, and No worries. I thought, why not make a mantra out of it: *it's beautiful, no worries. It's beautiful, no worries.* Then I thought, why not say *it's beautiful* on the inbreath and *no worries* on the out breath: breathing in beauty and getting rid of worry. Then I thought – cut it down to just *beautiful* on the inbreath, and *worries* on the out... and then I realised I was worrying too much about it.

Art in Melbourne

To give some feeling of the nest,
in my flashy hotel room,
I have placed two of my daughter's biroed pictures
on the doors of the huge television.
The doors remain shut.

Isabella has not long ago turned four.
Now, I know I may be biased,
but I consider these pictures to be fearfully superior
to any picture which might appear on the screen.
And these are by no means her best.

10 December 2007

Isabella played in her concert at Lauderdale House
about two weeks ago. Tony Yates, her teacher, dates
the piano about 1810. Says it is a fine one. The parade
of pupils came and played their pennyworth. Tony had
selected Isabella to close. Her first contribution was the
piece she has been learning by J.P. Rameau.

Rameau Swings

Jean Philippe, you had an
ear for music and a wig
for it too

Afterwards, you asked me how many I would give your pieces out of 10. For the second piece I gave you round about 9.2. You played it supremely. You hammered at the keyboard not only with your fingers but with your heart. And your eyes. And for your first piece I gave you 10. I have given you only one 10/10 before and that only lasted a little while and then went down to 9/10 because it had been Ten in the moment but then the moment moved on and the mark dropped to something top, but not tip top.

But this – it was 10. A Ten, full stop.

10 out of 10 for your Rameau.

Because, within the first few bars you made a fluff – and you *treated* it like fluff. Brushed it aside, like fluff upon the fleece, like fluff upon the ruff. To have played it perfectly would have got you 9.88 or 9.89.

Maybe as much as 9.93 even. But not 10.

Perfection is not 10 out of 10. That is reserved for perfectly dealt with imperfection. I only realised this, watching you play. For this you pull the full marks.

Next time of course, it will be more difficult, because it will be a little easier.

A letter from Giacometti to the subject of his narrow sculpture

My dearest Venice Woman,

Please do not take offence
because I have made you look like a gondola pole.
Yes, I have thinned you right down and my creation is
    not much of a likeness,
but I wish you to comprehend what it is that I am at.
In removing the fat,
I seek to portray your fundamental core.
Not that I am saying you ARE fat.
What I want to do,
is to bring your essential self through.
A distillation is what it boils down to.
My lovely piece of spaghetti

Love, Giacometti

*I saw a retrospective of Giacometti's work at The Scottish
Museum of Modern Art. I learned that at one point he
destroyed almost everything he had done. This is in keeping
with the figures he has left us, in which all but an essence is
thrown away.*

Mister Giacometti's
metaphorical machete
really cut his sculpted figures
down to size.
Up in Edinburgh's Modern
you can go and see the odd'un
standing long
and very thin
around the thighs.
What a guy!
Did you know that he wanted all his girlfriends
　　　shaven headed? Why? You may ask.
Why? This was his answer:
Because hair is a lie.

Dear Mum and Dad,

I am at the Edinburgh Festivities of Summertime
again. It's an inspiring place to visit. With the crags
above the City you're reminded of just how brief and
fragile are our days. People open out about the best of
shows to go to and the buses you can take from George
Street going up Lothian Road (11, 12, 16). Today I
took the 13 to the marvellous Museum of Modern Art,
where I go every year to inspect and reflect upon the
permanent collection. Every year those wonderful
exhibits make me vow to Wow the audience with
scenery and props of great invention. There was one
year, Dad, when I had one of your paintings as a
backdrop and as I lugged it from the venue at the end of
residing there, I felt so proud to have performed beside
your bright and atmospherical depiction, even though
the perspective's a bit wrong. And, Mum, please could
you knit me a long-sleeve jumper, for next year?

Love,
John

A plane-speaking man,
my brother

51 years and counting – a feat of engineering

You'll repair to your share of the aerodrome.
You're never at home in a no-fly zone.
Your lark is not that of the navy.
You are Marcel the excellent aviator.
The oil and the grease are your gravy.

Riddles

Riddle I

I fly.
I slip by. I get wasted. What am I?

I am time

Riddle II

Two in a person.
Four in a lemur.
I'm pulling your leg
for I'm your...

I'm your femur

Riddle III

I am a politician with an apology.
I'm an expert in heurology.
I'm an apple on a stair.

I'm a skinflint with change to spare.
No, I'm not common.
I am...

I am rare

Riddle IV

I'm the one before nine on a Sunday night out of
the capital.
First stop, Chichester.
A right rarity out of this station
for my South-coast destination
I'm...

I'm the 8:47 from London Bridge to Portsmouth

Riddle V

I flap, I fold
I often stand in sand
I rhyme with neck hair
I'm a...

I'm a deckchair

Riddle VI

I am alone
I am on the rocks
I am able to shed light for others
but deep inside me
there is a darkness
I am...

I am depressed

Keeping Mum and Dad

It's the song you used to sing about potatoes, Brother.
It's the wall up which you drove me when you did.
It's the little car you got me for my birthday.
It's a shame I came to find it
in the drawer before my birthday
on account of it was rather poorly hid.

Brother, we stood at the top of the town
and surveying your trousers of brown,
I said I had never before had the joy
of seeing you trousered in corduroy.
You said, 'You have now!'
Thinking backwards, when you were a boy,
didn't you have a windcheater made of the same?
In those days when you showed me the way
        to take aim
with a pea and a peashooter?
Those days of the bedroom we shared,
when your socks filled my nostrils
and I would object 'Will you stick them outside of
        the door
and not stinking near me on the floor?'
And then one day you acted the swine

and while I was sleeping, you placed your socks under
   my pillow
to give me a shock when I woke on the morrow.
Those days of the comics we eagerly spread
the comics that crossed the ravine
that was in-between your bed and mine
and dad would come in
and draw open the curtains
and in came the flame of the sunshine.
The colours which patterned those curtains of
   boyhood
are colours I cannot recall,
but what was depicted on that bedroom wallpaper's
   clear in my knowing:
A rowing boat, over and over repeated
tied up in long grass by the shore
with an island a way off,
I wished to go out and explore.

Though I didn't go then
I am rowing there now
cutting through waves like I'm driving a plough.
I arrive at the land
and I stand in the sand
and then Mum helps me tie up my boat
and Dad is about
he is dressed as a Scout
And he says to me, 'Here is a groat.'

Joan of Arc joins us
and so does the bark of the dog she calls Johann
     Sebastian.
'Sorry I'm late,' she says – 'Nowhere to park.'
I tell her, 'Your armour is covered in rust.'
Joan says, 'Quite honestly, I should be dust.'
How she's learned English it isn't discussed.

She's holding the dog-lead and also a pebble,
the pebble she throws at the flood
and the dog paddles out through the watery spread
and comes back from the wet with a spud.
There's some kind of kiosk,
there's Dad at the counter,
he says he is ready for trade.
The briny it couldn't be calmer.
Mum says, 'An old suit of armour, I dreamed of,
to have there, upgrading the hall,
but a shiny barometer's all that we had

that and the hat that went over the face
of your daddy who went out to work in the world
with his arm curled around his attaché case.'
I cannot hear Mummy so well,
because I've got my ear to a shell.

A Roman comes by,
he is ancient and I
say, 'Do sit in this chair if you wish.'
The Roman relaxes, forgets about taxes,
one more of Joan's pebbles goes splish.
The Roman is dressed in unusual gear,
on his head is some bread just a crust.
'Time is the ogre' he says in his toga,
his knowledge of English, it isn't discussed.
And Mum says, 'You should wear a hat or a hanky
or maybe a spotty cravat.'

The Roman nods off in the deckchair
and I think, 'So what sort of gratitude's that?'

The wind's in the palms of the trees.
I ask Dad for a bread roll with cheese,
if possible, sliced and not grated.
Dad said, 'You didn't say please.
Though, in fairness, you dropped to your knees.'
He hands me a bread roll with cheese,
grated, not sliced
but it's ever so reasonably priced.
All that it costs is a groat
and Mum says to check on my boat.
I'm unable to hear her too well,
because I've got my ear to a shell.
Mum says, 'You don't need a shell
when you're standing right next to the swell of
      the ocean.'
And Dad says, 'Your mother is right.'
And they sing and their harmony's tight.
And it's out on the ocean
together they tread
and they head for the distance
dancing, elated,
distributing bread
to the birds of the ocean with words of delight.

A dalek appears
with a pair of false ears,
I think it is time I was going.
I get in my boat and start rowing.
I go over the watery spread,
back to our bedroom and back into bed.
Back from the sand and the rocks.
Back from the world beyond distance and clocks
and back to the stink of your horrible socks.

Brother, without both our mother and father
I just don't know where I would be.
It's just as well I'm in possession of parents
and both of them live
in my poetry.

Peace, love and potatoes

Wed in 1944
my mother
kept on peeling from the pick
of the potato sack,
with the occasional knack
of getting their jackets off
all in one piece.
Quite a trick. A quiet feat.
Like her and Dad's feeling for each other:
uninterruptedly alive
and complete.

Beach of promise

Here's the sunlight.
Here's the land.
Here's the castle
made of sand.

Here's the lighthouse
there's no keeper
every year the climb got steeper.

Sand of beach
and beach of promise,
watched by quiet eye of lighthouse.
Towering up above the foam,
light house
sweet home.

The pebbles are skimming.
The people are swimming.
They're lunging and limbing.
They plunge and they slice.

There's Punch and there's Judy,
they're fighty and feudy,

while others are giving
parental advice:

> Don't get sand in your eyes,
> but in between your toes
> and the hairs of your nose
> and in the wrinkles of your elbows,
> the sand's alright.

The open-top buses
are one of the pluses
going down to the seaside's
the best of descents.

My bucket and spade is
for digging to Hades
the lav for the ladies
is next to the Gents.

The sea it is seething
the toothless and teething
they're all of them breathing
the oceany air.

On land and in lotion,
the sand and the motion.
Devoid of devotion,
we haven't a prayer.